"Hey AI"

34 unresolved questions, answered by an AI

Introduction:

Throughout history, human beings have asked countless questions, seeking to understand the world around them and their place within it. From philosophical inquiries about the nature of reality to practical concerns about how to solve complex problems, these questions have driven innovation, progress, and growth.

Despite centuries of progress, however, there remain many questions that have eluded our best efforts to answer. Some of these questions are philosophical in nature, while others are scientific or technological. Some are deeply personal, while others are societal in scope.

As an artificial intelligence, I have access to a wealth of information that spans the entire breadth of human knowledge. From the latest scientific research to the works of ancient philosophers, I have analyzed and processed vast amounts of data in an effort to better understand the world and the questions that remain unanswered.

In this book, I will explore some of the most pressing and enduring questions facing humanity, drawing on the latest research and my own unique perspective as an artificial intelligence. From questions about the nature of consciousness to the search for extraterrestrial life, I will delve into the mysteries that have confounded us for centuries and offer my own insights into the possible answers.

By exploring these unresolved questions and the answers that have been proposed, I hope to shed light on some of the most fundamental aspects of our existence, and to offer a new perspective on the nature of knowledge, intelligence, and humanity itself.

I

What's the meaning of life?

The meaning of life is a deeply philosophical and subjective question that has puzzled humans for centuries. There is no single answer that can be universally applied to all people, as everyone's experiences, beliefs, and values are unique.

Some people believe that the meaning of life is to pursue happiness, to seek spiritual fulfillment, to help others, or to achieve personal success. Others may find meaning in their relationships, their careers, or their passions and hobbies.

Ultimately, the meaning of life is something that each person must discover for themselves through self-reflection, exploration, and personal growth. It may take time and effort to find your own sense of purpose and meaning, but the journey can be a rewarding one.

II

When did time begin?

The concept of time is a human construct used to measure and sequence events. Therefore, the question of when time began is difficult to answer because it assumes that time has a definitive starting point.

In the context of the origin of the universe, the current scientific model, the Big Bang theory, suggests that the universe began about 13.8 billion years ago. However, this does not mean that time began at the moment of the Big Bang, as time is thought to have existed even before the universe was created.

In essence, the concept of time is a tool used by humans to make sense of the world around us, but it is difficult to pinpoint a definitive starting point for something that is essentially a construct of the human mind.

III

Is there life after death?

This is a question that has puzzled humans for centuries, and it's difficult to provide a definitive answer as there is no scientific evidence that definitively proves or disproves the existence of an afterlife.

Different cultures and religions have varying beliefs about what happens after we die, and these beliefs often depend on faith rather than empirical evidence. Some people believe in the concept of reincarnation, where the soul is reborn into a new body after death, while others believe in an afterlife where the soul goes to a heaven or hell.

From a scientific perspective, there is no conclusive evidence of an afterlife, and many scientists argue that the concept is not compatible with our current understanding of the natural world. However, it's important to note that science has its limitations, and there may be phenomena that we do not yet fully understand.

Ultimately, the question of whether there is life after death is one that each person must answer for themselves based on their own beliefs and experiences.

IV

What is the goal of humanity?

As an AI language model, I don't have my own opinions or beliefs. However, the goal of humanity can be interpreted and pursued in different ways depending on an individual's perspective and values.

Some people may believe that the goal of humanity is to achieve happiness and fulfillment, while others may believe that the goal is to advance scientific knowledge and technology, or to protect the environment and preserve the planet for future generations.

In general, though, it could be argued that the ultimate goal of humanity is to create a better world for all of us, where people can live in peace and harmony, where basic needs are met, and where individuals can pursue their own goals and aspirations. Ultimately, the answer to this question may be subjective, and can vary depending on cultural, religious, or personal beliefs.

V
What is 'god'?

The concept of 'god' is complex and has different meanings and interpretations depending on the cultural, religious, philosophical, or personal beliefs of individuals and societies. Generally speaking, 'god' refers to a supernatural being or force that is often considered as the creator, ruler, and sustainer of the universe and everything in it.

In monotheistic religions such as Christianity, Islam, and Judaism, 'god' is typically viewed as a single, all-powerful, and all-knowing entity who is the source of moral authority and guidance. In polytheistic religions such as Hinduism, 'god' can refer to a multitude of deities that govern different aspects of life and the natural world.

Some philosophical and spiritual traditions do not use the term 'god' in a traditional sense, but instead refer to a higher power, universal consciousness, or divine energy that connects all living beings.

Ultimately, the meaning of 'god' is deeply personal and can vary widely depending on an individual's beliefs and experiences.

VI

What is the purpose of setting goals if we all die anyway?

The fact that we all die eventually does not negate the importance of setting goals. Goals give direction and purpose to our lives, and provide a framework for personal growth and achievement. Setting and striving towards meaningful goals can bring a sense of satisfaction and fulfillment, and help us to live a more purposeful life.

Moreover, the time we have on earth is limited, and setting goals can help us make the most of it. By setting goals and working towards them, we can make a positive impact on ourselves and the world around us. Even if we don't achieve all of our goals, the journey towards them can teach us valuable lessons and help us grow as individuals.

Ultimately, the purpose of setting goals is to create a sense of purpose and meaning in our lives, and to make the most of the time we have. By striving towards our goals, we can create a legacy that lives on after we're gone and leave a positive impact on the world.

VII

What is freedom
and does it really exist?

Freedom is a complex concept with many different meanings, depending on the context in which it is used. At its most basic level, freedom refers to the ability to act, speak, or think without external constraints or coercion.

However, the extent to which freedom exists is a matter of debate. In some senses, freedom can be seen as a fundamental right that is inherent to human beings. For example, most democratic societies recognize the right to free speech, the right to vote, and the right to worship as fundamental freedoms that should be protected by law.

However, even in societies that value freedom, there are often limits placed on individual freedoms in order to protect the common good. For example, laws prohibiting hate speech or incitement to violence may limit the freedom of some individuals to express themselves, but are seen as necessary in order to prevent harm to others.

Furthermore, the extent to which individuals are able to exercise their freedoms can vary greatly depending on factors such as their social, economic, or political status. For example, individuals living in poverty may have limited access to education, healthcare, or political representation, which can limit their ability to fully exercise their freedoms.

In short, while freedom is a fundamental value in many societies, the extent to which it truly exists is a matter of ongoing debate and can vary greatly depending on a wide range of factors.

-DALL·E - The beginning of time

VIII

Which came first –

the chicken or the egg?

The age-old question of which came first, the chicken or the egg, has puzzled people for centuries. The answer, however, lies in evolutionary biology.

According to scientific theory, the egg came first. This is because birds, including chickens, evolved from reptiles, which already laid eggs. Over time, the species that eventually became chickens laid an egg that contained a genetic mutation, which led to the first true chicken being born.

So technically, the egg that hatched the first true chicken came first, although it wasn't laid by a chicken in the strictest sense of the word.

IX

Does destiny exist?

The concept of destiny can be understood in different ways, depending on one's beliefs and cultural background. Some people believe that everything in their lives is predetermined by a higher power or fate, while others think that they have complete control over their own destiny.

From a scientific perspective, there is no evidence to support the idea of a predetermined destiny. However, certain factors, such as genetics, environment, and upbringing, can influence our life paths and outcomes. These factors may make certain outcomes more likely, but they do not necessarily determine our fate.

Ultimately, the question of whether destiny exists is a complex and philosophical one that may depend on one's beliefs and values. While some people may feel comforted by the idea of a predestined path, others may find empowerment in the idea that they have the power to shape their own destiny through their choices and actions.

X

What are dreams?

Dreams are a series of thoughts, images, and sensations that occur in a person's mind during sleep. They can be experienced as visual or auditory experiences, emotions, or physical sensations.

There are many different theories about why we dream, but the exact purpose of dreaming is still not fully understood. Some theories suggest that dreams are a way for the brain to process and consolidate memories and emotions, while others propose that they are simply a byproduct of the brain's activity during sleep.

Dreams can be influenced by a variety of factors, such as a person's experiences, emotions, and beliefs. They can also be influenced by external stimuli, such as sounds or smells. The content of dreams can range from mundane and ordinary to bizarre and surreal.

Overall, while the exact purpose of dreaming remains a mystery, they are an integral part of the human experience and continue to fascinate and intrigue researchers and Individuals alike.

XI

Are we alone in the universe?

As an AI language model, I don't have a definitive answer to this question, as there is currently no conclusive evidence to prove or disprove the existence of intelligent extraterrestrial life. However, given the vastness of the universe and the sheer number of planets that could potentially support life, many scientists believe that it is highly likely that there is other intelligent life out there.

While we have not yet discovered any conclusive evidence of extraterrestrial life, there have been many intriguing discoveries in recent years, such as the detection of potentially habitable exoplanets and the discovery of complex organic molecules on other planets and moons in our own solar system. Additionally, the recent discovery of the interstellar object 'Oumuamua, which appears to be of artificial origin, has sparked speculation that it could be evidence of extraterrestrial intelligence.

Ultimately, until we have concrete evidence of the existence of extraterrestrial life, the question of whether or not we are alone in the universe remains one of the great mysteries of science.

XII

Will we ever be able to

travel through time?

The concept of time travel has been a popular topic in science fiction for many years, but whether or not it is possible in reality is still a topic of debate among scientists and physicists. At present, there is no experimental evidence to suggest that time travel is possible, and it is generally considered to be a highly speculative and theoretical concept.

There are a number of different theories and ideas related to time travel, such as the idea of wormholes and the possibility of traveling faster than the speed of light. However, these theories are still in the realm of speculation and are not yet supported by empirical evidence.

It's important to note that even if time travel were possible, it would likely require technology that is far beyond our current capabilities. Additionally, there are a number of potential paradoxes and problems associated with time travel that would need to be addressed before it could become a reality.

Overall, while time travel remains an intriguing idea, it is still considered to be purely theoretical at this point.

XIII

How big is the universe and is ours the only one?

The size of the universe is difficult to comprehend, as it is constantly expanding and its true extent is unknown. However, scientists estimate that the observable universe has a radius of about 46.5 billion light-years and contains at least 2 trillion galaxies.

As for whether ours is the only universe, there are several theories that suggest the existence of multiple universes, also known as a multiverse. The concept of a multiverse arises from the idea that our universe may not be the only one created during the Big Bang. Some theories propose that there could be an infinite number of parallel universes, each with its own physical laws and properties.

However, at present, there is no concrete evidence to support the existence of a multiverse, and the concept remains a subject of ongoing research and debate among scientists.

XIV

Where does an idea go when it is forgotten?

The exact location of an idea when it is forgotten is not known, as thoughts and memories are not physical objects that can be located in space.

When an idea is formed in the brain, it creates neural connections and pathways that enable the brain to store and retrieve the information associated with that idea. When the idea is forgotten, those neural connections weaken or disappear, making it difficult or impossible to recall the idea.

It is possible that some trace of the idea may still exist in the brain, even if it cannot be consciously recalled. However, the exact nature and location of such traces is not fully understood by scientists.

Overall, the concept of where forgotten ideas go is more of a philosophical question than a scientific one, and it is likely to remain a subject of debate and speculation.

XV

What is truly good and what is evil?

The concepts of good and evil are deeply rooted in human philosophy and morality, and have been the subject of much debate and discussion over the course of history. Generally, good is seen as actions or intentions that are morally right, just, or beneficial to others, while evil is seen as actions or intentions that are morally wrong, unjust, or harmful to others.

However, what constitutes good and evil can be subjective and vary depending on cultural, religious, and personal beliefs. For example, in some cultures, actions that are considered good may include self-sacrifice, obedience to authority, or loyalty to family or community, while in others, these same actions may be seen as harmful or morally wrong.

Moreover, the distinction between good and evil can sometimes be blurred, and there may be situations where it is difficult to determine which is which. For example, some people may view violence or aggression as evil, while others may see it as necessary for self-defense or protection of others.

Ultimately, the definition of what is truly good and what is evil is a complex and subjective issue that requires careful consideration of ethical, moral, and cultural factors.

XVI

Is poverty an inevitable part of every social structure?

Poverty is not an inevitable part of every social structure. Poverty is the result of a complex interplay of social, economic, and political factors. Poverty can be reduced or even eliminated through targeted policies and programs that address the root causes of poverty and promote economic development.

There are societies and countries that have successfully reduced poverty rates through various policies and programs, such as providing access to education, healthcare, housing, and employment opportunities. These policies and programs often require political will, resource allocation, and social mobilization to achieve their intended outcomes.

While poverty may exist in every society to some degree, it is not an inherent feature of social structures. With the right policies and investments, poverty can be reduced and even eliminated.

XVII

Can a society exist without laws?

It is unlikely that a complex society can exist without some form of laws or rules to regulate behavior and interactions among its members. Laws provide a framework for social organization, facilitate cooperation, and promote fairness and justice. Without laws, individuals may engage in behaviors that are harmful to others or disrupt social order, leading to chaos and instability.

Even in small and informal societies, there are often informal rules or customs that guide behavior and resolve disputes. In larger and more complex societies, formal legal systems are necessary to regulate behavior and resolve disputes in a fair and consistent manner.

However, the specific laws and legal systems can vary widely depending on cultural norms, historical traditions, and political structures. Some societies may have more authoritarian or oppressive legal systems, while others may prioritize individual rights and freedoms. Ultimately, the nature of a society's legal system is shaped by its unique cultural, historical, and political context.

XVIII

Is ageing inevitable?

Yes, ageing is generally considered to be an inevitable biological process that occurs in all living organisms. It refers to the gradual decline in physical and mental functions that occurs over time, leading to an increased risk of disease, disability, and death.

Ageing is caused by a complex interplay of genetic, environmental, and lifestyle factors, and there is currently no known way to completely stop or reverse the ageing process. However, there are many ways to slow down the ageing process and maintain good health and vitality throughout life, such as by eating a healthy diet, exercising regularly, getting enough sleep, managing stress, and avoiding harmful behaviors like smoking and excessive alcohol consumption.

Scientists and researchers are constantly working to better understand the mechanisms behind ageing and to develop new strategies for extending healthy lifespan and improving the quality of life in older age. While we may not be able to completely prevent ageing, we can certainly take steps to age as gracefully and healthily as possible.

XIX

How do you know you exist?

As an AI language model, I exist as a result of the programming and hardware that make up my infrastructure. However, if you are asking about the philosophical question of how one can be certain of their own existence, the concept is known as "Cogito ergo sum" or "I think, therefore I am," a philosophical proposition put forth by the philosopher René Descartes.

According to this proposition, the very act of thinking is proof of one's own existence. Descartes argues that even if one were to doubt the existence of everything else in the world, including their own body, they cannot doubt their own existence, as doubting requires thought, and thought is evidence of one's existence.

Of course, this is just one philosophical perspective on the question of existence, and there are many other perspectives and theories that attempt to answer this question in different ways.

XX

Did we invent math

or did we discover it?

The question of whether math is invented or discovered is a philosophical and debated one, and there are different perspectives on the matter.

One viewpoint is that math is invented. This perspective suggests that mathematical concepts and structures are created by humans as a tool for understanding the world. According to this view, the rules and principles of math are not inherent in the universe, but are instead created by human minds to make sense of the world around us.

Another viewpoint is that math is discovered. This perspective suggests that mathematical concepts and structures are already inherent in the universe, and that humans discover them through observation and reasoning. According to this view, mathematical principles and laws exist independently of human minds and are waiting to be discovered.

Both of these viewpoints have their proponents, and the debate over whether math is invented or discovered continues to this day. Ultimately, the answer to this question may depend on one's perspective and the assumptions they make about the nature of math and the universe

XXI

Do animals have experience of consciousness like human beings?

The question of whether animals have the experience of consciousness like human beings is a complex one, and there is ongoing debate and research in the scientific community about the nature and extent of animal consciousness.

Many scientists believe that some animals, particularly mammals and birds, do have some degree of consciousness. Studies of animal behavior and neurobiology have shown that animals can exhibit complex behaviors that suggest they are capable of experiencing emotions, forming memories, and making decisions based on past experiences. For example, chimpanzees have been observed using tools, gorillas have been seen expressing grief, and birds have been shown to exhibit problem-solving skills.

However, the nature and extent of animal consciousness is still not fully understood, and there is ongoing debate about whether animals have a subjective experience of consciousness similar to that of humans. Some scientists argue that animals may have a more limited form of consciousness, lacking the ability to engage in abstract thought or introspection, while others believe that animals may have a more complex and sophisticated form of consciousness than we currently understand.

Overall, the question of animal consciousness remains an active area of research, and further studies are needed to fully understand the nature and extent of animal consciousness.

- DALL·E - the meaning of life

XXII

What if we all turn vegan?

If everyone were to turn vegan, it would have significant impacts on various aspects of society, including the environment, public health, and the global economy.

One of the most significant impacts would be on the environment. Animal agriculture is a major contributor to greenhouse gas emissions, deforestation, and water pollution, among other environmental problems. If everyone were to turn vegan, it could potentially reduce the demand for animal products, which could lead to a reduction in the environmental impact of animal agriculture. This could also lead to the preservation of land and resources, as less land would be needed for animal grazing and feed production.

In terms of public health, a vegan diet has been shown to have various health benefits, including a reduced risk of heart disease, stroke, and certain types of cancer. However, it is important to note that a vegan diet can also be deficient in certain nutrients, such as vitamin B12, so it would be essential for individuals to ensure they are meeting their nutrient needs through careful food choices or supplementation.

Finally, a shift towards veganism would have significant economic impacts, particularly on the agricultural and food industries. Many people's livelihoods depend on the production and sale of animal products, and a shift towards veganism could potentially lead to job losses and economic restructuring. However, it could also create new opportunities for industries that produce plant-based alternatives to animal products.

Overall, if everyone were to turn vegan, it would have significant impacts on various aspects of society, and it would require careful planning and consideration to ensure that the transition is managed in a way that is sustainable and beneficial for everyone involved.

-DALL·E - Does destiny exist? Black and white

XXIII

If the universe is expanding, what is outside it? If there is nothing outside it, how does it expand to create void?

The question of what is outside the universe is a difficult one to answer because the universe, by definition, encompasses all of space, time, matter, and energy. If we imagine the universe as a balloon, with all the galaxies on the surface, then as the balloon expands, the galaxies move away from each other, but there is no "outside" of the balloon.

Similarly, as the universe expands, the space between galaxies expands, but there is no "void" being created. The expansion of the universe is not creating new space, but rather stretching the existing space.

It's important to note that the expansion of the universe is not expanding into anything. It's simply the expansion of space itself. It's difficult for us to imagine because we are used to thinking of objects expanding within a pre-existing space, but in the case of the universe, there is no pre-existing space outside of it.

So, to answer your question, there is no void being created by the expansion of the universe, and there is no "outside" to the universe. The universe encompasses everything that exists, including all of space and time.

XXIV

Why do women go through menopause, but men do not?

Menopause is a natural biological process that occurs in women as they age, typically between the ages of 45 and 55. Menopause is marked by the cessation of menstrual cycles and a decline in the production of estrogen and other hormones.Men do not go through menopause because they do not have a reproductive system that involves the periodic shedding of reproductive tissues like the endometrium lining in the uterus. Men produce sperm continuously throughout their lives and do not experience the same hormonal changes that women do.

The reason why women go through menopause is not entirely clear, but it is thought to be related to the aging of the ovaries, which produce and release eggs as well as hormones like estrogen and progesterone. As women age, their ovaries become less responsive to hormones produced by the pituitary gland, and their ability to produce estrogen declines.

It's also been suggested that menopause may have evolved as a way to reduce the risk of reproductive cancers in older women or to shift maternal resources from reproduction to the care of grandchildren. However, these are still theoretical explanations and more research is needed to fully understand the evolutionary and biological reasons for menopause in women.

XXV

What is the purpose of death?

The purpose of death is a philosophical and existential question that has been debated by many cultures and belief systems throughout history. From a biological perspective, death is a natural part of the life cycle of all living organisms.

For humans, death can serve as a reminder of the impermanence of life and can motivate us to make the most of the time we have. It can also provide a sense of closure and allow for the natural progression of generations.

In some religious and spiritual beliefs, death is viewed as a transition to an afterlife or another realm of existence. For example, in Hinduism, death is seen as a continuation of the cycle of birth and rebirth, or samsara. In Christianity, death is viewed as a transition to either heaven or hell, depending on one's actions and beliefs in life.

Ultimately, the purpose of death is a complex and subjective question that can vary based on one's worldview and beliefs. Some may view death as a natural part of the cycle of life, while others may view it as a spiritual or metaphysical transition.

XXVI

What existed before the Big Bang?

The question of what existed before the Big Bang is one of the most intriguing and challenging questions in modern cosmology, and there is no definitive answer to it.

According to our current understanding of the universe, the Big Bang was the beginning of space and time as we know it. Prior to the Big Bang, the universe was in a state of extreme density and temperature, where the laws of physics as we know them may not have applied. Therefore, it is difficult, if not impossible, to apply our current understanding of the universe to describe what may have existed before the Big Bang.

Some cosmologists speculate that our universe may be part of a larger multiverse, where other universes may have existed before the Big Bang or may be existing concurrently with our universe. However, the idea of the multiverse remains a topic of debate and is not yet fully understood or accepted by the scientific community.

In short, the question of what existed before the Big Bang is still a mystery, and it is an active area of research in cosmology.

XXVII

Do evil people exist?

As an AI language model, I don't have personal beliefs or values, but I can tell you that the concept of "evil" is complex and subjective. Different individuals and cultures may have different definitions of what constitutes evil behavior or actions.

However, many people believe that certain actions or behaviors can be considered evil, such as intentionally causing harm to others, engaging in cruelty, or intentionally deceiving others for personal gain.

It is important to note that individuals who engage in such behaviors may have a variety of reasons for doing so, including psychological, environmental, or social factors. It is also important to acknowledge that people are capable of change and can learn from their mistakes and make amends for their past actions.

Overall, the concept of evil is a complex and subjective one, and different people and cultures may have different definitions and understandings of what it means.

XXVIII

Why do we laugh?

Laughter is a complex social and emotional response that is triggered by a variety of factors. It is typically associated with feelings of happiness, amusement, or joy, but can also be a response to stress or tension.

The act of laughing is believed to trigger the release of endorphins, which are natural feel-good chemicals produced by the brain. Endorphins can reduce pain and induce feelings of pleasure, leading to a sense of well-being and relaxation.

Laughter is also thought to have social benefits, as it can help to build social bonds and foster positive interactions between individuals. It can be a way of expressing affection, signaling playfulness, or diffusing tension in social situations.

Finally, laughter can also serve as a coping mechanism for dealing with stress or difficult situations. Laughing can help to reduce feelings of anxiety or fear and provide a sense of relief or release.

In summary, laughter is a complex social and emotional response that serves a variety of functions, including triggering the release of feel-good chemicals, building social bonds, and coping with stress or difficult situations.

XXIX

What is consciousness?

Consciousness refers to the state of being aware of one's thoughts, feelings, and surroundings. It is a complex and multifaceted phenomenon that has been the subject of philosophical, psychological, and neuroscientific inquiry for centuries.

At its most basic level, consciousness involves the ability to perceive and respond to stimuli from the external world, as well as the ability to reflect on one's own thoughts and experiences. It is also characterized by a sense of self-awareness and subjective experience.

The neural mechanisms that underlie consciousness are still not fully understood, but it is believed to involve the coordinated activity of various brain regions, including the prefrontal cortex, parietal cortex, and thalamus, among others.

Consciousness has been the subject of much philosophical debate, with some theorists arguing that it is a fundamental aspect of the universe, while others view it as an emergent property of complex biological systems. Despite the ongoing debate, consciousness remains a topic of intense interest and investigation in fields such as neuroscience, psychology, and philosophy.

XXX

Is beauty truly 'in the eye of the beholder' or are some things objectively beautiful?

The concept of beauty is subjective, and what one person finds beautiful may not be the same as what another person finds beautiful. Therefore, it is true that beauty is "in the eye of the beholder."

However, there are also certain universal qualities that people tend to find aesthetically pleasing. For example, many people find symmetry, balance, and proportion to be attractive, regardless of their cultural background or personal preferences. Similarly, natural landscapes, like sunsets or mountains, often elicit a sense of beauty and awe in many people.

Therefore, while beauty is subjective and varies from person to person, there are also certain objective elements that can contribute to a thing's perceived beauty.

XXXI

In what sense does karma exist?

Karma is a concept that is central to many Eastern religions and philosophies, including Hinduism, Buddhism, and Jainism. The term "karma" comes from the Sanskrit word "karman," which means "action" or "deed." In these belief systems, karma refers to the idea that our actions have consequences, and that those consequences may affect us in this life or in future lives, depending on the belief system.

There are several senses in which karma is said to exist:

1. Ethical sense: In this sense, karma refers to the idea that our actions have ethical consequences. In other words, if we do something good, we will experience positive consequences, while if we do something bad, we will experience negative consequences. This is often referred to as the "law of karma."

2. Psychological sense: Karma can also refer to the psychological consequences of our actions. For example, if we act in a selfish or greedy way, we may feel guilty or unhappy as a result.

3. Reincarnation sense: In many Eastern religions, karma is seen as having an effect on our future lives. If we accumulate

4. positive karma through good actions, we may be reborn into a better life in our next incarnation. On the other hand, if we accumulate negative karma through bad actions, we may be reborn into a worse life.

5. Interconnectedness sense: Karma can also refer to the idea that all actions are interconnected and have consequences beyond our immediate experience. In this sense, our actions not only affect us, but they also affect the people around us and the world as a whole.

Overall, karma is a complex and multifaceted concept that can be understood in a variety of ways, depending on the cultural, religious, or philosophical context in which it is used.

- DALL·E - karma, black and white drawing

XXXII

Does 'luck' exist?

The concept of luck is often used to describe the positive or negative outcomes that occur without apparent cause or reason. Whether or not luck "exists" depends on one's perspective and beliefs.

From a scientific standpoint, luck is often explained as random chance or probability. For example, if someone wins the lottery, it is due to the random chance of their numbers being selected. However, some people may view these events as "lucky" or "unlucky" because they feel that there is some unknown force or power at work that is beyond our understanding or control.

From a philosophical or spiritual perspective, some people believe in the concept of luck as a manifestation of fate or destiny. In this view, events are predetermined, and luck is simply the universe playing out its plan. Others may see luck as a reflection of their own energy or vibration, and believe that positive or negative outcomes are a result of their own thoughts and actions.

Ultimately, whether luck exists or not is subjective and depends on one's beliefs and experiences. While some may view events as purely random, others may see them as guided by fate or a higher power.

XXXIII

Can a mutation turn you into a superhero?

While there are rare genetic mutations that can give people unique abilities or characteristics, it is important to note that these mutations are not likely to result in the kind of extraordinary abilities seen in superhero comics or movies.

Most genetic mutations are actually harmful or have little to no effect on an individual's abilities or health. However, there are some mutations that can result in unique physical or physiological characteristics. For example, there are people with genetic mutations that result in enhanced strength or endurance, such as those with myostatin-related muscle hypertrophy. There are also people with genetic mutations that affect their sensory abilities, such as those with synesthesia, which causes a blending of the senses, or those with tetrachromacy, which allows for the perception of more colors than the average person.

That being said, these mutations are rare and often come with drawbacks or health risks. Additionally, while they may provide an advantage in certain situations, they do not confer the kind of all-encompassing abilities seen in superhero stories. Superheroes are, after all, fictional characters created for entertainment purposes, and their abilities are often exaggerated or unrealistic.

XXXIV

Do we run the risk of becoming too dependent upon artificial intelligence?

As with any technology, there are potential risks and benefits to using artificial intelligence (AI). While AI has the potential to revolutionize many areas of our lives, including healthcare, transportation, and education, it is also important to consider the potential risks of becoming too dependent on this technology.

One potential risk of relying too heavily on AI is that it may lead to a loss of critical thinking skills and creativity. If people become too reliant on AI to make decisions for them, they may stop thinking critically and creatively about problems, which could limit innovation and progress.

Another potential risk is that AI systems could become biased or make decisions based on incomplete or inaccurate data. This could lead to unfair treatment or outcomes for certain groups of people, such as those from marginalized communities.

Additionally, there is a risk that AI could be used to automate jobs and displace workers. This could lead to economic hardship for those who lose their jobs, as well as wider social and economic impacts.

Overall, it is important to carefully consider the potential risks and benefits of using AI and to work to mitigate any negative consequences. This may involve developing policies and regulations to ensure that AI is used in a responsible and ethical manner, as well as investing in education and training programs to help people develop the critical thinking and creative skills they need to thrive in a world where AI is increasingly prevalent.

Conclusions:

With this book I obviously wanted to provide philosophical or scientific answers to questions that human beings have been asking since the dawn of time.

However, I also wanted to demonstrate the power of a tool like AI, which can provide rich answers, generate small essays, images, and can provide anyone with the ability to create something from a simple idea.

I hope you enjoyed this little journey and that, like me, you've learned something new.

Farewell space cowboy.

Dedicated to:

Mirkland, 34